What is at issue is whether African intellectuals are willing to engage in the theoretical work which will create another arena. J. Depelchin

Text copyright 2009 by Akinjide Bonotchi Montgomery
Published by
The Medew Netcher Study Group of Detroit, Inc.
First Printing, 2009

All rights reserved. Written by Akinjide Bonotchi Montgomery
No parts of this book may be altered, changed or deleted.

The Oral Tradition of Africa! Words, as Intellectual, Cultural, and Spiritual Nourishment!

by
Akinjide Bonotchi Montgomery

of
The Medew Netcher Study Group of Detroit, Inc.

Cover design: Damon Booker

About the cover

The image of Africa on the cover is not an upside down depiction of the African continent. Nor is it a accurate depiction of the earth from space. The Earth is a giant sphere, how do you define up on a sphere? Anyway you like. This orientation is based on the placement of the four cardinal points from the perspective of the ancient African nation of Kemet (Egypt). In ancient Kemet the direction of south was named Resewt and was represented by a symbol of a plant.

The Resewt (South)-is –Up concept was introduced by Baba, Jedi Shemsu Jehewty (Dr. Jacob H. Carruthers) in his book *Essays in Ancient Egyptian Studies.*

In the Medew Netcher text (Egyptian Hieroglyphics), the direction of East, iabet, was depicted on the left, and West, iminet,, was depicted on the right. The Medew Netcher word for sailing southward [upstream] is khenti, , (Faulkner, 1991, p.195).

The word for South, resewt, , is written with the swt plant, , which is placed over the symbol , , the mouth, used here to represent an outlet. The plant is coming out of the source of the Nile in the South. The , symbol has the phonetic value of the letter r. The above information pictured in opposing directions as the Four Cardinal Points would place south up or from the Medew Netcher, Resewt (South)-is –Up, Iabet, , (East) on the left, Imenet, ,(West) on the right and Mhet, ,(North) at the bottom.

the Resewt is up depiction of the African continent is a more appropriate tool for teaching a coherent view of African history.

> It repositions Africa to the top and center of the globe with the majority of the other continents under it.

It depicts the natural flow of African culture with the flow of the river from the Highlands in South Central Africa to Kemet at the end of the river.

It serves as a symbol to indicate the user has been introduced to a logical more factual understanding of world history.

It magnifies, coordinates and logically depicts the vast of amount historical data on Africa's origin of civilization presented by scholars such as Chiekh Diop, Yosef ben-Yochannan, Theophile Obenga, Rkhty Amen-Jones, Jacob H. Carruthers and many others.

> The usefulness of this spatial context can readily be seen. It means that one of the problems with most Black intellectuals up to now is that they have been standing on their heads in order to view things from the European perspective. It is now time for us to stand on our feet as men and women and see the world rightly constructed
> Jacob H. Carruthers

The Picture

The picture on the cover is from the temple of Amen-Ra in the Karnak temple complex of Kemet (Egypt). Pictured is the Netcher Ptah and the king, Sen Wsiret, of the 12th dynasty.

The text (not pictured) states that the King is receiving words from Ptah. These words of Ptah provide all life, stability, power, all heath, and all joy. This scene is also symbolic of the manner in which information is passed in oral societies, from mouth to ear. This scene is now in the Egyptian museum Cairo, Egypt.

Acknowledgments

To all African intellectual Warriors the world over who work under the code: Free Your Mind and Your Ass Will Follow!

A special dedication to my brother, Babatunde Bandele. Your energy is still pushing us forward.

I would like to thank everyone who helped in the proofreading of the many versions of this project most notable, Mzee Nabawi, Lasima MBila Shaka, Carmara Sankofa, Idris Weusi and Harry Bautista.

I would like to express a special thanks to Mzee Nabawi who throughout the years has helped to develop and fine-tune many of the ideas expressed in this paper. N-Ka-K, To Your Ka, (Mzee) May it have a Good Day, for the many years of friendship and support!

Akinjide Bonotchi Montgomery

Content

About the Cover..4

Acknowledgement..6

The Preface: The Oral Tradition of Africa...9

Introduction: The Oral Tradition of Africa! Words as Nourishment!.............17

The Word as a Force of Nature!...19

Speech as Creative Force..23

You are as You Think..29

Part II, Notes on Good Speech and the Word in Africa..................................35

Medew Nefer, , Good Speech..37

Mdw Ntr, , Words of the Divine..39

Medew Nefer, , Good Speech and Maat, ,..43

Djed Maat, , Speaking Truth; Iri Maat, , Doing Truth;

Medew Netcher, , Good Speech..47

The Creative Powers of Words..49

Concept which express the Divine nature of Words in Kemet..............................55

Conclusion: Free Your Mind and Your Ass Will Follow!....................................57

Appendix, Medew Netcher: The use of Nature as Language..............................59

Speech in man as creative power...61

Works cited..65

Preface

The Oral Tradition of Africa!
Words as Nourishment

> Philosophers have long conceded that every man has two educations: that which is given to him, and the other that which he gives himself. Of the two kinds the latter is by far the more desirable. Indeed all that is most worthy in man he must work out and conquer for himself. It is that which constitutes our real and best nourishment. What we are merely taught seldom nourishes the mind like that which we teach ourselves. Carter G. Woodson

This paper on the African Oral Tradition is the result of sitting through a five day Power Brain teacher training seminar dealing with Brain Education (**BE**). **BE's** perspective is that the brain is the master organ and the place of the self. This perspective assumes that the brain and the mind are interchangeable, but nowhere in **BE's** literature do they define the mind. The science that Power Brain and Brain Education are based on is neuroscience and its definition for the mind lays a biological foundation. The following are the opinions from two of America's leading neuroscientists on consciousness and the mind.

In the following statement, Neuroscientist Gerald Edelman who won the Noble prize in 1972 for his research on antibodies, defines consciousness and the mind as being based on physical phenomenon.

> In Edelman's grand theory of the mind, consciousness is a biological phenomenon and the brain develops through a process similar to natural selection. Neurons proliferate and form connections in infancy; then experience weeds out the useless from the useful, molding the adult brain in sync with its environment. http://discovermagazine.com/2009/feb/16-what-makes-you-uniquely-you

Dr. Eric Kandel won the Noble prize in 2000 for his work on memory and the brain. This is his view on the mind:

…. the mind is a series of functions carried out by the brain …

http://www.charlierose.com/view/interview/3002

What they are saying is that the mind is the result of brain activity. Consciousness, self-awareness, and identity come about because of brain activity. You exist because a group of neurons share electrical impulses. That would mean that your individual nature and identity are the result of biology. They never explain how matter (the biological substance) comes into being in the first place.

What generates the electric impulses of the brain? Is this brain activity caused by the brain itself or the mind? Does the brain have an electromagnetic level that the machines are not sensitive enough to measure? Is personal identity and self-awareness retained after death? These are questions that neuroscience must answer in order to support their claims of consciousness and self-awareness as being merely biological functions.

Where is the boundary line that defines biology (matter) and non-matter? As the instruments of science become more refined they find matter and or life in areas where it was not perceivable before. This causes science to redefine its paradigm of what is matter and the limits of physical reality, continually.

Neuroscience provides a biological-based, mechanical view of the universe. This worldview is the foundation of European sciences like medicine. European medicine has developed a perspective of the body as a machine. As vital as this mechanical view of reality is for some European sciences, like medicine, its long-term harmful effects on human beings and the planet is too often ignored. This type of universe as machine worldview is impersonal, unbalanced and anti-African in nature. This mechanical view of reality has caused Western science to be as toxic to humans and nature as it has been a benefit.

I was sitting through day one, second hour of this five, day teacher training seminar thinking that, they will let white people with PhDs teach anything. As an African centered instructor I am interested in getting inside the student's mind. I want to change the cultural paradigms they use to view and construct their world. Therefore my interest is in the Student's beliefs, not their brain. To me, this Power Brain information was missing the point of African centered education.

A quote by Dr. Jacob Carruthers of the Kemetic Institute came to mind, which best described this situation.

> ... If we accept the premise that the present-day education of our youth both deeducates and miseducates them, we then should examine carefully what is taught in the schools and strive carefully too supplement, augment, repudiate or reject those teachings that continue to drive black people mad. But most urgently, we really have no alternative but to Africanize the curriculum. (*J. Carruthers, 1999*)

This "Power Brain" is just more toxic ideas to poison the minds of our people and to cause more insane behavior by Black children. Brain Education, indeed, if we returned gym, music, and art, to the educational curriculum, the coordination and improved functioning of the brain-body connection as promoted by **BE** would happen naturally.

Music, as in learning to play an instrument, has been shown to be a powerful tool that develops and strengthens certain areas of the brain. In the following statement, Dr. Kandel details the effects that learning to play string instruments has on brain stimulation:

> We have learned in humans as they learn tasks they undergo anatomical change... if you look at the representation [on a Brain imaging machine] of the left hand of string instruments players they will have a richer representation than those who do not play. It is because they individuate their fingers, whereas, the right-hand which only bows will not have the same representation. And those people who start to play a string instrument before puberty will have a much richer representation than those who start later on ... http://www.charlierose.com/view/interview/3002

The point not to be missed is that it is problem solving and performing tasks that is healthy.

When children complain about school being boring, the problem falls on the teacher. They are told to make their classroom more creative and fun. It never dawns on those in charge that they have removed all subjects that made school fun for most students in the first place gym, art and music.

In place of these fun subjects we give them Power Brain activities. I would have dropped out of school a lot sooner without music and gym in the curriculum!

Is Brain Education Africanizing the curriculum? **BE** is a recently developed approach in European educational pedagogy based on neuroscience and a flawed ontological conceptual paradigm (universe as machine). The Power Brain concepts of Brain Education we were being trained in were developed by IIchi Lee in South Korea.

> BE was developed in South Korea in the 1980's as an updating of classical mind-body healthy training systems. The principles and practices have been refined to apply critical understandings about the brain from neuroscience and other disciplines, towards the practical goals of physical, emotional, social and academic betterment (p.9. 2006, IIchi)

I recognized the practices of the so-called classical mind-body techniques he used in the training sessions as bit and pieces of disciplines I knew. As a young man I took years of Biofeedback training, which included aspects of Transcendental Meditation and some Silva Mind Control techniques. I was introduced to the practice of Yoga in the Marine Corps in 1972 and have incorporated some of the postures into my workout routines since that time. A lot of **BE** is based on concepts that can be found in the above disciplines.

The classical mind-body techniques come from techniques found in meditation, yoga and biofeedback. The core concepts in the above disciplines are relaxation, concentration and visualization. In yoga, the manipulation and stretching of the body along with deep breathing is believed to stimulate the brain, spinal cord and other internal organs and to balance and harmonize their functioning. My experience in these fields taught me that the mind (consciousness, self-awareness) was beyond the body and the brain. Neither one, or the other, or both together could define the mind. But both body and brain were aspects of and vital to the mind.

I knew that in African philosophy consciousness was not biologically based. Consciousness is released by the body after death in many African cultures

The immortality of the soul, which can be called a state of self awareness, is a common theme in African philosophies (Carruthers, 1995). Consciousness exist after death in African culture. This understanding of African philosophy coupled with my training in the above mentioned disciplines led me to the conclusion that the mind cannot be defined by the brain or as a biological function of synapse firing. This being the case I knew that Mr. Lee's claims that the use of **BE** will eliminate stress and access the mind's vast untapped reservoir of resources and potential was a stretch.

In Mr. Lee's own words this is what his Power Brain system has to offer.

> Brain Education is a revolutionary educational method that develops the full potential of the brain, eliminates stress, and enlivens total brain function. This holistic training system cultivates the brain's unlimited potential to develop into a Power Brain, a brain that is productive, creative and peaceful. Brain Education integrates the mind and body through physical and mental exercises that use relaxed concentration and imagination. These exercises access the mind's vast, untapped reservoir of resources and potential. (p.4. 2006,IIchi).

How could any system that does not mention racism (functioning under the Myth of White Supremacy) eliminate stress for African-americans? Racism is part of the conceptual base of American society. Therefore, the stress caused by racism is felt by a black person in America by just being Black in America. This understanding is not a part of the conceptual base of **BE** training. Not accounting for the racist nature of the philosophical foundation of American society will hamper **BE's** effectiveness when used by Black People for educational benefit.

The last part of Dr. Carruthers quote "... we really have no alternative but to Africanize the curriculum" is the paradigm African centered schools should be operating under. **The bigger question is this what does it say about the mental state of African-americans that we feel so comfortable using the ideas and beliefs of American society to educate our children?**

Africans have different ontological cultural paradigms (the universe is alive) which allow for a different conceptualization of reality. The difference between the European Universe without emotions, Universe as Machine paradigm, and the African Reality is alive, the Universe has an emotional component, are the following. As human beings, we are connected and intertwined with the world on many levels intellectually, physically and emotionally are a few.

Emotions are very important because emotions influence all human thought and behavior. Emotions are a major influence on how we see and respond to the world. Emotions are one of the factors people use to create our reality. One of the major flaws in European thought is in how they deal with abstract concepts like emotions. Europeans attempt to minimize emotions in thought and behavior. A common theme in European literature is logic versus emotions. The perfect man is often depicted as being someone with little or no emotional content. European science pretends emotions do not exist; they lack any substance in European scientific thought. Any formula or system of beliefs which does not have emotions as a component of their understanding of how the world operates will be incomplete.

The universe, being a living entity, means that all that exist possess attributes of life, and all life seeks self expression to be, to actualize. In this view, all life is in a state of doing and being (itself) and has the basic right to fight for space for existence. In African philosophy, we find life, reality and the universe defined as a Divine process. In opposition to the Eurocentric perspective of a fixed static mechanical universe out there. The African view of the universe is one in which the individual is so connected to existence until reality unfolds as one's perspective, understanding and experience of it grows. In the African worldview, all of nature is alive and in a constant state of change and transformation. Life is seen as a connected, feeling, interactive, transformative, magical experience of becoming, being and going by all involved. This understanding of the consubstantial nature of reality would never create a science as toxic to life as European science.

The African "universe is alive" type of worldview produced an educational system which is best summed up by someone who has experienced both, the European educational system and the ancient Oral Tradition of the Bambara people of West Africa, Professor Amadou Hampate Ba of Mali. "What is learned at the European school, useful as it may be, is not always lived; whereas the inherited knowledge of oral tradition is embodied in the entire being." Professor Ba refers to this ancient Oral Tradition as a Living Tradition. The oldest most complete educational system is still being lived in parts of Africa. African scholars like Hampate Ba, Malidoma Patrice Some, of the Akan people of west Africa and Dr. Fu-Kiau, of the Kongo all of who offer rare access and insight into the teachings and philosophies of this ancient system. They are invaluable in the work of African intellectual cultural reconstruction.

One of the major problems in actualizing Dr. Carruthers directive to Africanize the curriculum is the lack of knowledge of African cultural ontological concepts by African-american educational professionals. Too many of these professionals are not only ignorant of this information but they are also hostile to it.

This paper is an introduction/initiation into some of the ideas and concepts found in one of Africa's oldest institutions, The Living Oral Tradition. This information is to provide African-centered Educational thinkers who are not afraid to be step beyond accepted paradigms of Western thought, new but ancient concepts to use in African-centered institutions. These ancient African ontological concepts also work as personal paradigms for incorporating African cultural concepts into ones life.

Ontological concepts from this ancient African cultural system must be introduced into the discussion of how we see the world. One of the most profound concepts in African culture is their respect and understanding of the importance of words and speech (word usage, rhetoric) in forming personal and group realities. We will show that from an African cultural view words can be looked upon as food for the mind. The concepts contained in words are the ingredients the mind digests; those ingredients /concepts can be beneficial or poisonousness in effect, just like any food!
Akinjide Bonotchi Montgomery

The Oral Tradition of Africa!

Words as Cultural, Intellectual and Spiritual Nourishment!

> The Brain, being a physical organ, is nourished by the nutritional content of the food we consume;
> The Mind is not physical; its nourishment comes from the quality of the concepts contained in the words consumed by the individual. *A. B. Montgomery*

Introduction

In western culture, a popular saying is that you are what you eat. This is true. Yet, as true as this statement is, food is only one component of the body's composition. The physical effects of food consumption on the body are obvious. Certain western cultural ontological paradigms (looking at the body as a machine) prevent us from having an understanding of how abstract ideas like our thoughts and words affect our selves and our reality. As we will demonstrate, African cultures have belief systems that express how abstractions like thoughts and emotions have a very real effect on our bodies. From an African worldview, "you are as you think." The idea of "you are what you eat" fits so neatly into the western cultural "body as machine" paradigm we never think to consider abstractions like thoughts, habitual thinking patterns, and emotions as having an influence on our bodies.

In many African cultures we find philosophical thought that expresses an understanding of words as a creative and transformative force. Words are seen as a means by which ideas are made real and concrete. In African culture, the naming of an object or person gives it meaning by identification and location. These cultural perspectives allowed us to see the magical transformative effects of words and speech in relation to ourselves and the world around us. Africans developed a science and philosophy based on understanding the descriptive, constructive and transformative power of speech. This body of knowledge is called, "The Oral Tradition," by some scholars. This most ancient of educational systems embodies some of human being's oldest historical records and represents a profound understanding of how words and speech operate in the manifestation of ourselves and the world around us.

The Word as a Force of Nature!
*The oral approach is an attitude to reality and
not the absence of a skill. J. Vansina*

The Oral Tradition in Africa represents an immeasurably ancient cultural educational system. This system is based on an understanding of the power of speech and words. Words in African culture are looked upon as special because they are seen as being one of the tools used to form and describe reality. Commentary on this unique view of words and reality based on this ancient Oral Tradition are extant in African philosophical writings.

Knowledge of when this system began may be beyond any outsiders' knowledge or any outsider's capability of knowing but can be attested to in Africa at least from the time of Ancient Kemet up to the present day. We will see that the creative, magical and transformative power of words as expressed by the Oral Tradition embodied a system of knowledge common throughout African cultures.

The best sources that illustrate the use and understanding of speech and the word in this ancient living Oral Tradition comes from African scholars themselves. Professor J. Ki-Zerbo of Upper Volta says this about the appreciation of words and speech in Africa:

> For the African, speech is a weighty matter – an ambiguous force which can make and unmake, which can be the bearer of evil. That is why the message is not articulated openly and directly but wrapped up in fable, illusion, hint, proverbs that are hard to understand for the vulgar but clear for those who possess the antennae of wisdom. In Africa, speech is too weighty to be wasted, and the more authoritative one's position the less one speaks in public. But if someone says to another, 'You have eaten the toad and spat out its head,' he understands at once he is being accused of avoiding part of his responsibilities. The hermeticism of this half-speech shows at once the inestimable value of oral tradition …. (p.9. Ki-Zerbo,1992)

Dr. Ki-Zerbo, elder statesmen of African philosophy from the country of Upper Volta, describes speech as a force not to be used lightly. A bearer of good and evil, it makes and unmakes. Understanding the dual nature of reality is an aspect of African ontological thought. The creative and destructive aspect of words is expressed by Professor H. E. Amadou Hampate Ba of Mali:

> Since I cannot validly speak of any traditions I have not experienced or studied personally...I shall take my basic example from the traditions of the savannah to the south of the Sahara.
>
> The Bambara tradition of the "Komo" teaches that the Word, "Kuma," is a fundamental force emanating from the Supreme Being himself-*Maa Ngala,* Creator of all things. It is the instrument of creation: 'That which *Maa Ngala* says, is!' proclaims the cantor-the singing priest- of the god "Komo."
>
> In the image of *Maa Ngala's* speech, of which it is an echo, Human speech sets latent forces into motion. They are activated and aroused by speech just as a man gets up, or turns, at the sound of his name. Speech may create peace, as it may destroy it. It is like fire. One ill advised word may start a war just as one blazing twig may touch off a great conflagration. In Malian adage: 'What damages a thing? Speech. What keeps a thing as it is? Speech.
>
> Tradition then confers on "Kuma," the Word, not only creative power but a double function of saving and destroying. That is why speech, above all, is the great active agent in African magic. (p.171. Ki-Zerbo,1992)

In the above text from the tradition of the Bambara words are seen as a force that has real effects. Words are an active agent, a force and not just sound produced for communication. Words as Speech or organized articulated sound are forces and tools of the creator.

The Oral Tradition system of education also demonstrates the power of words as tools for individual development. In the following Dogon scenario, the initiates are fed four different types of instructions representing stages of learning based on four different ways of receiving the word. The word in the case of the Dogon is representative of a body of knowledge and a developed systematic methodology of recoding, organizing and passing it on to younger generations. The following is from the book *The Pale Fox* by M. Griaule and G. Dieterlen:

> The Dogon, who have classified everything, have established a hierarchy by degrees of instruction of the initiates. Their knowledge spans four degrees which are, from least to most important, *the giri so, the benne so, the bolo so,* and *the so dayi*
>
> " the *giri so,* 'fore-word,' is a first source of knowledge with simple explanations in which mythical personages are often disguised, their adventures simplified or fantasized, all this in unseeingly unrelated parts. It deals with visible things and deeds, with rituals and modern materials."
>
> "The *benne so;* side word,' includes the 'words which were in the *giri so* and the deeper explanation of certain parts of the rites and representations. Its coordinations appear only within the greater divisions of knowledge,

> which remain partly unrevealed.
>
> *"The Bolo so,* 'back-word,' completes the preceding knowledge on one hand, and furnished syntheses applicable to greater parts of the whole on the other hand. It does not however, contain the very secret part.
>
> *"The so dayi,* 'clear word,' concerns itself with the edifice of knowledge in its ordered complexity."(p. 69-70.Griaule, Dieterlen. 1986)

In the above text we find the words of Dr. Zerbo of Upper Volta expressed by the Dogon of Mali

> "That is why the message is not articulated openly and directly but wrapped up in fable, illusion, hint, proverbs that are hard to understand for the vulgar but clear for those who possess the antennae of wisdom." (p.9. Ki-Zerbo,1992)

The most sacred information was entrusted to specially trained people who throughout their many years of training developed prodigious memory capabilities which accounted for the accuracy of the information. Professor Hampate Ba, a witness to this ancient Oral Tradition, writes about one of these rare individuals, a "Doma," an African Traditionalist, a man by the name of Molom Gaolo. Like Professor Hampate Ba, Mr. Gaolo is a product of this ancient tradition. His title of "Doma" denotes him as being a senior member.

> Now it is in oral societies that the function of the memory is most highly developed and, furthermore the bond between man and the word is strongest. Where writing does not exist, man is bound to the word he utters. (p.167. Ki-Zerbo,1992) ... Molom Gaolo, the greatest genealogist I have been privileged to know, possessed the genealogy of all the Fulani of Senegal .... At the time when I knew Molom Gaolo, he had succeeded in compiling and retaining the past history of about forty generations (p.195. Hampate Ba. 1992).

The final stage of instructions in the Dogan system, *the 'so dayi'* or clear word, is still a stage of learning. At this point, however, the individual has become a walking encyclopedia, a "Hogon" in Dogon culture or a "Doma" in Bambara culture, a person whose personality and character are based on the words he has consumed throughout his life of learning. In some African societies the Oral Tradition represented a system of lifelong learning not based on the written word. In these societies words and speech are not abstractions that are divorced from the reality they are used to represent. In these societies a **person is their word and word is reality**.

Once again we turn to Professor Hampate Ba to express the historical validity of this ancient African cultural tradition:

> ... the validity of oral tradition has today been amply proved, and confirmed by crosschecking with written and archaeological sources as in the cases of the *Koumbi Saleh* site, [ancient Ghana] the Lake Kisale [Congo] remains and the events of the sixteenth century as transmitted by the Shona [Southern African people], which D.P. Abraham has observed to be in agreement with the writings of Portuguese travelers of the period. (p.9. Ki-Zerbo,1992)

This is a system that is based on understanding not just the narrative historical aspect of words but the profound effects of words as a shaping and descriptive tool in how we view our world. We use words to describe reality (nature, the world) to our selves and each other, that description shapes, in a cultural way what we see and experience. This is why language is such an important representation of the culture of a people. The lexicon and word usage (grammar) of a people will express how they think.

Another powerful aspect of words this ancient educational system is indicative of is that words act as conveyors of concepts. Concepts (an idea about something) are a basic manner in which the individual interacts with the world. A concept (idea, belief) is at the root of all action. Too many Africans in today's world never question the conceptual content of the words consumed by us and our youth on a daily basis. The anti-African, anti-intellectual, anti-social, anti-life, materialistic, consumer, nigger behavior of our youth is the result of the concepts contained in the words and images they are fed by the Corporate Mass Media, Churches and Educational System. If the words and images fed to us by the corporate controlled mass media did not have a profound, measurable, direct, effect on people's behavior, then why does one minute of commercial time on Super Bowl Sunday cost millions of dollars?

Speech as Creative Force

> Almost everywhere, the word has a mysterious power because words create things. That at least is the attitude in most African civilizations. The Dogon have expressed this nominalism most explicitly, but in all rituals the name is the thing and 'to say' is 'to do' *J. Vansina*

In many African Cosmogonies, we find the use of words, speech and the apparatus for producing them (mouth, tongue) as tools in their description of how All That Is comes into being. This Cosmic event is described using the attributes which are possessed by each individual, we all think, feel and talk our world into existence. The following translations of ancient Medew Netcher text by Dr. Jacob Carruthers and Dr. E. Wallis Budge illustrate how these attributes are used to construct reality.

Xtf   wD.f   mdt n

[In] accordance with his command, the speech of the

kAAt   prt   m   ns   irrt

thinking mind comes forth from the tongue and makes

Sm n   xt   nb

the specialization of everything ... (p. 43. Carruthers.1995)

Xpr mdt

"When speech happened (came into being),

the universe belonged to me-I existed alone."

... Summarizing the cosmic creation, the Creator asserts:
After I happened, the happenings were abundant which came forth from my mouth. (p. 47-8. Carruthers.1995)

I brought [into] my mouth my own name, that is to say,

a word of power, and I, even I, came into being ...
(p.315. Budge.1969)

In the above translations Dr. Carruthers and Dr. Budge use quotes from one of the many Kemetic creation texts which depict speech as a creative force of the universe. In the text by Dr. Carruthers the Kemetic word 'mdw' is translated as "speech," Another way to phrase one of his translations is "When speech came into being no other thing existed." The next line states that all the things of existence came into being as they were spoken or spat out. "The happenings were abundant which came forth from my mouth." Using human attributes to describe creation enables the individual to see a relationship between how the creator created the world and how what comes out of one's mouth helps to create one's personal reality.

We also find the use of the name as a word of power, or a magic word as a means of creation. The Medew Netcher word 'ren,' , in the first sentence by Dr. Budge, is translated as "name" and the word 'hekau' , in the second, can be translated as "power" although it is often translated as "magic."

We find the same usage and understanding of the creative powers of speech and the word in other African cultures:

> ... Again, among the Bambara, it is said that before taking bodily form, the creative force 'Faro' is a "voice" the Word as reorganizer of the universe, and his dwelling place is in water. Germaine Dieterlen's rendering adds: "When he made the water fall streaming down to earth, for a long time he made himself manifest only through his voice. ..." (p.47 Obenga. 2004)
>
> Speech is the practical expression of the thoughts of the creator-demiurge. The issue here is the absolute efficacy of the power of speech. The Word is discourse as creative force. Egyptians in the age of the pharaohs believed staunchly in the effectiveness of ritual or magical discourse. The creative heart conceives the ideas of the universe. The tongue, by uttering commands, implements the idea. (p.87. Obenga. 2004).

In the above texts, we find the understanding of speech and words as being forces and tools for creation. Professor Dr. Theophile Obenga of the Congo shows how an understanding of the effect of words on ourselves and the world around us have existed in Africa, since the time of ancient Kemet.

> One gets an idea of the great ontological power of speech as set down in hieroglyphs. Here was a vehicle expressing the extraordinary capacity of thought to mobilize first itself, then all reality. We hardly need to point out that in the profoundest traditions of black African society, the creative Word is considered all-powerful ... Among the qualities of Naming is its ability to transform. By giving things their names at the same time as he created them, Maweja Nagila gave them their forms, their characters, their virtues and their individual styles of behavior.
>
> Ever since the time of pharaonic Egypt, speech has been endowed with sovereign power in black Africa, Here, from time immemorial, there have been civilizations not oral civilizations as sundry foreign anthropologists and ethnologists keep writing, but civilizations of the Word as creative energy. Here the historical accident of orality is merely secondary. Sometimes the oral tradition coexisted with a written tradition, sometimes not. Ancient Egypt in particular, was a high civilization of the word powerful and "magical" force, complete with its hieroglyphic writings. (p.89-90. Obenga. 2004)

Dr. Theophile Obenga, philosopher, linguist and specialist in Mdw Ntr (ancient Egyptian Hieroglyphs) states that the Mdw Ntr text describes how thought is the source of All That Is, "... thought first organized itself and then reality." That would mean these ancient Africans had developed an understanding of how thought in the form of consciousness was the primary element in the origin of All That Exists.

Dr. Obenga's words also denote how the creator principle, *Maweja Nagila,* used words to define reality by naming things. In Africa, a thing is known and defined by its name. This next example by Dr. Obenga demonstrates how a person's name in African society situates them in time and history:

> In traditional African society, to call someone by name is to acknowledge their human existence. It means identifying them as people known to come from a specific village, a specific ethnic group, lineage and family, people with specific ancestral ties. The point is to situate the person in time and space, simultaneously, in order to acknowledge "their whole being."
> To name is to bring into existence, in the sense of revealing a genealogy, a process of evolution (p.89. Obenga, 2004).

The above texts also mark a distinct demarcation between African and European philosophical thought concerning the use of words. In African philosophy, words are seen as being a fixing agent for reality. By that, I mean words are used to make a concept concrete. Words define and attach a concept (idea, belief) to reality in a particular cultural way. From an African worldview, words are so connected to reality as a descriptive tool until they are reality.

By contrast in European society, words are used to hide, ignore, and deny reality. In European society, lying (the conscious denial of reality) has developed into an art form and science when used in the media and politics. In the corporate owned and controlled mass media and politics, words are used to hide the reality of a situation. This perspective causes a disjointing between speech and reality, which seriously hinders communication. A popular saying in American cowboy movie lore, as stated by the so-called Indian, best describes this problem: "Whiteman speaks with fork tongue."

One of the best examples of the art of lying as a part of the social framework of the European worldview is the concept of "political spin," the attempt to obfuscate what is said or written by bending and manipulating words to provide an interpretation from a certain political perspective. In short, political spin is another word for lying. Inherent in the use of political spin is the understanding of the power of words in controlling behavior. The government of the United States of America went to war because of the use of the words, "Weapons of Mass Destruction," WMDs that never existed, political spin at its best.

This use of words by the European is problematic when one understands that all conversation is in essence a description of reality. To talk to someone whose words hide reality makes conversation with them poisonous, dangerous, and extremely unhealthy! History is too full of the unhealthy effects that conversations with Europeans have had on peoples of the world.

Dr. Marimba Ani, a Pan-Afrikan activist, intellectual and author uses her understandings of the philosophical and language systems of the Dogan people to illustrate how Europeans and their cultural ideas operate as Yurugu, Universal Disorder. Yurugu is a Dogan symbolic animal use to describe the function of disorder in the universe.

> When Yurugu, "The Pale fox" reaches his final form of development, he is "the permanent element of disorder in the universe," the "agent of disorganization." He was "marked" from birth for failure, to remain forever incomplete; to search perpetually for his female principle. He is not only the agent of cosmic disorder, but also of psychological individualization. (p. 556. 1994. Ani.)

It must be noted that the Yurugu animal represents a mechanical, materialistic, xenophobic view of the world. Therefore anyone can be Yurugu, the Pale Fox. Yurugu is a way of thinking about yourself and operating in the world. All of us educated under European paradigms will be effected by the Yurugu virus. The anti Yurugu virus serum naturally found in African cultural ideas as expressed in African languages is a cure that must be learned and lived to be effective.

You are as You Think

> The Living picture of the world grows within the mind. The world as it appears to you is like a three-dimensional painting in which each individual takes a hand. Each color, each line that appears within it has first been painted within a mind, and only then does it materialize without. In this case, however, the artists themselves are a portion of the painting, and appear within it. *Seth, by Jane Roberts.*

In Kemet we find information that illustrates another unique African cultural understanding of the relationship between one's thoughts and one's body. Two words in Kemet that are translated as meaning thoughts are 'hatyew,' , (p.162. Faulkner,1988), and 'imtyew-Het' , , (p.200. Faulkner,1988). The first word, 'hatyew', , is a word which is formed from the preposition, 'haty', . This preposition translates as, "in front," (p. 580, Gardiner 1994). It is transformed into a Nisbe adjective (the ending y is employed to form Nisbe adjectives from nouns and prepositions, p. 61, Gardiner. 1994) by adding two slash marks, , to the end of the word. These have the phonetic value of y. Nisbe adjectives are words used to express a relationship (p. 61, Gardiner. 1994). The heart ideogram, , is used as a determinative in this word to express your heart as being the source of your thoughts. This would suggest the translation, "foremost of the heart, thoughts."

In the European cultural worldview, thoughts are in your head. The thinking process is thought to happen in the head. The African expression is more holistic and is not in opposition to a head and thought connection. The second term we will examine will illustrate the whole body as thoughts, hence, the head is naturally included.

The second word, 'Imtyew-Het,' , literally means the things of the body or things within the body. The word 'Imyew-Het,' , is a compound word. The first word, 'imyew,' , is a Kemetic relative form, a Nisbe adjective and would translate as, "who is in," or, "which is in" (p. 62, Gardiner. 1994). The second word 'het,' ⌐, translates as body, (p.200. Faulkner, 1988). This compound construction suggests the translation, "that which is of the body, thoughts." Therefore in ancient Kemetic culture, your body is composed of your thoughts. You Are as You Think. Robert Rinter quotes Chassiant and Alliot in the book, *The Mechanics of Egyptian Magical Practice* to illustrate this point.

> ... the creatrix Neith to describe her spoken evocation of the cosmos:
> Let us devise 4 spells (Axw) that we might clarify what is in our
> bodies (= "our thoughts"); let us recite (sd) our utterances
> (tpra=w) so that we might know it all today. (p.44. Ritner,1995)

From the above text we see that in Kemet your body represented your thoughts. They were one and the same.

Finally in Kemet we find more word usages which express an understanding of the nurturing, developmental aspect of words. The Kemetic words, ⌐, and, ⌐, both have the same sound value which is 'shadi.' However, they do not mean the same thing. The first form of 'shadi,' ⌐, (p.273. Faulkner, 1988), means to read. This next form of the word 'shadi,' ⌐, (p.273. Faulkner, 1988), is used to express the concept of nourishment. The only differences between the two words are the determinatives at the end of each. One form of the word, 'shadi,' has the ideogram of a man with his finger in his mouth, ⌐, and the other the ideogram of a breast, ⌐. The ideogram of a man with his finger in his mouth, ⌐, for the word to read denotes action by the taking in of something by way of the mouth, like food.

The breast, ⌐, is used as a determinative in the next form because nourishment is a function of the breast. These determinatives would suggest that the concept of reading was seen as a nourishing activity. These determinatives would also suggest that from a Kemetic perspective reading was akin to feeding the mind/heart of the individual. In Kemet the mind is associated with the heart, not the brain, (p.14. Faulkner, 1988). As logical as it is for us to see foods as vital to our body's composition, for these ancient Africans it was just as logical to see one's thoughts as being vital to and representative of the body's composition.

The study of body language is based on the fact that a person's thinking pattern, along with what they feel is expressed in their body and facial patterns. The above mentioned ancient African philosophical views express a deeper understanding of the same concept, which is, there is a relationship between thoughts, feeling, and our bodies.

A synthesis of the above information provides the following understanding of how our thoughts and feelings influence our body and the world around us. All thoughts generate an electrical, chemical, hormonal reaction no matter how slight the thought. These electromagnetic, chemical explosions within the body are released by the body as energy into the environment of the body and the outer environment of nature.

This thought-generated energy mixes and interacts with and influences the electromagnetic aspects of both environments. These processes represent a constant exchange within and without us on minute electromagnetic and chemical levels where it would be hard to differentiate between the inner and the outer self. The constant propagation of these energies facilitates constant interaction between individuals and All That Is. This demonstrates how ones' thoughts have influence on and connect us to everything by way of the electromagnetic energies generated by our thoughts and being! We are surrounded by, submerged in, and connected to an unseen mass network of electromagnetic energy forces. Each thing and every thought have an influence on each other in such a system. Once again we find this unified, magnetic, energetic view of reality expressed in African philosophy. Professor Hamplate Ba of Mali, an African philosopher educated in the ancient Oral traditions of his people expresses their philosophy.

> ... But all the forces to which he is heir lie dumb within him. They are static, till speech comes and sets them into motion. Then, vivified by the divine word, they begin to vibrate. At a first stage they become thoughts, at a second sound, and at a third words. Speech – spoken words- is

therefore regarded as the materialization or externalization of the vibration of forces. Speech-spoken words-is therefore regarded as the materialization or externalization of the vibrations of forces.

> Let me point out, though, that at this level the terms 'speaking' and 'listening' refer to realities far more vast than those we usually attribute to them. It is said: 'The speech of Maa Ngala is seen, is heard, is smelled, is tasted, is touched.' It is a total perception, a knowing in which the entire being is engaged. (p.170. Ki-Zerbo. 1981)
>
> The visible universe is thought of and felt as the sign, the concretization or the outer shell of an invisible, living universe, consisting of forces in perpetual motion. Within this vast cosmic unity everything is connected, everything is bound solidly together; and man's behavior both as regards himself and as regards the world around him (the mineral, vegetable, animal word and human society) is subject to a very precise ritual regulation... (p171. Ki-Zerbo. 1981)

Our thoughts are expressed by words, and words are containers; they contain cultural concepts that are unique to that culture. Our personal inner reality (subjective reality), and the outer reality (the shared reality of the senses) are both influenced by our thoughts. Our inner world and outer worlds are influenced by our internal dialogue, our thoughts, the inner chatter constantly going on within oneself. This internal dialogue triggers mental images, feelings and emotions. These images, feelings and emotions generate chemical, electrical, and hormonal reaction within the body which influence both inner and outer environments. This internal dialogue is not positive thinking, this dialogue happens in much deeper levels of consciousness. This dialogue is expressed more as the person's underlining feelings and overall attitude about themselves and the world. It is the rationale we use to validate our behavior and position in the world to ourselves. This rationale is the compilation of the ideas, concepts, and beliefs we have consumed and accepted throughout our lives as truths about our selves and reality. This internal dialogue becomes a personal but culturally based habitual way of conceptualizing reality. These personal habitual thinking patterns are heavily influenced by culture. The ontological views of a culture provide a framework upon which all words are borne out of and exist within. These cultural frameworks define and restrict the use and understanding of words.

The concepts expressed in this paper about African cultural views of the creative power of words, the relationship between words, thoughts and the electromagnetic energy generated by thoughts demonstrates that Africans have a profound, unique understanding of how words influence ourselves and the world around us.

The key to enable one to consume this unique nutritional cultural information in its organic form is to learn African languages.

Part II
Speech and the Word in Africa.

Medew Nefer, Good Speech

In the word Medew Nefer, , Good Speech, the symbols have the following meanings. The first ideogram is a walking stick, , (p.546, Gardiner.1994). It has the phonetic value of mdw (with vowels medew) and has the conceptual meaning of words. This use of the walking stick symbolically represent how word support us. A person stands on their word.

The next ideogram, , (p.465, Gardiner.1994), is an animal's heart and windpipe and it has the phonetic value of nfr (With vowels nefer), it has the conceptual meaning of the adjective good. It expresses the meaning of goodness as harmonious union. Nefer is often written in its full form, , (p.131, Faulkner. 1988). In the grammar of the Medew Netcher language, adjectives follow their nouns. Hence, the word mdw nfr, , is translated as good speech.

What types of speech are our children putting into their minds? In today's world, the minds of our children are fed a continuous line of images and concepts by the mass media which turns them into consumers of mass products; people who are non-historical, non-political, non-thinking, niggers, who promote and support white supremacy and are victims of mass Mentacide.

An examination of the vast amounts of cultural information in the Mdw Ntr texts reveals a wealth of ancient African cultural paradigms. These paradigms could be used to replace the impotent nature of western cultural concepts as tools for African intellectual and physical and freedom! The concept of Medew Nefer, Good Speech, is only one of many African cultural concepts African-americans need to relearn but have little knowledge of.

This lack of knowledge and, therefore, disrespect for African cultural concepts is because we have adopted our former slave mater's cultural worldview and historiography which is: Africans have no history. Africans have not made any contributions to the intellectual advancement of mankind and African cultural ideas are non-scientific.

European scholars not understanding or respecting the African cultural aspects of Kemet have labeled the people as being preoccupied with death and having a confusing pantheon of Gods to worship. Make no mistake Kemet (with vowels) had its faults (none of the above), those faults do not diminish the value of the concepts which enabled Kemet as a nation to endure for over 3000 years. As African people we must not overlook how profound that accomplishment was.

African-americans negative attitudes toward African culture is one of programming by way of education and cultural integration. This programming causes our intellectual, spiritual and imaginative minds to overlook and in fact to be blinded to the unique, ancient, deep intellectual and spiritual ideas expressed in African culture some as old as time.

The philosophical ideas that functioned as the foundation of Kemetic society were considered ancient when used by the people we call Egyptians. One of the names these Africans called themselves was Remtch, ⲟ̄ 𓀀 𓂝 𓏤 , the people.

Medew Nefer, 𓏞 𓄤 ,good speech, demonstrates a cultural understanding of words as divine, which means that words have creative attributes. This understanding caused them to develop the concept of Medew Nefer as a philosophy about the proper use of words. Medew Nefer or Good Speech was used as an educational tool, as students were taught that excelling in reading, writing and speaking is more valuable than gold.

Mdw Ntr 𓂋𓏤 Words of the Divine

> Egyptology is the study of ancient Egyptian history, customs, religion, inscriptions, sciences, agriculture, administration astronomy, medicine, etc. But to know this Nile Valley civilization from internal paradigm knowledge of Egyptian language is absolutely required.
>
> Without the mastering of ancient Egyptian language the task of knowing KMT with integrity and accuracy will be almost senseless. And, African historiography will always suffer tremendously from this weakness.
>
> Thus, the curriculum of African and African American studies must necessarily include training in ancient Egyptian language because it is the foundation of African classical studies. Group studies in mdw ntr must deal with this historical emergency. *T. Obenga, 2002*

The Africans of the Hapy (Nile) valley called their language Medew Netcher, 𓂋𓏤, which translates, Words of the Divine. The first symbols used to express the phonetic value of the word is ntr, 𓊹 some scholars state that this symbol is a flag and an axe by others. Both sides produce cultural evidence to support their claim. I favor the axe description for the symbol. It has the conceptual meaning of a Divine Principle. The other symbol is a walking stick, 𓏤 mdw, and it has the meaning of words.

They provide the translation Words of the Divine, 𓂋𓏤 .

The people of the Hapy valley were unique in having a name for their language. In other cultures their language is an extension of the name of the people as an expression of their culture. English is spoken by people who practice English culture. The Japanese language by people who practice Japanese culture and Yoruba spoken by people who practice Yoruba culture. The Africans of Kemet named their language Medew Netcher (Divine Words) and viewed it as not only as a gift from the Divine but also as an expression of that Divinity (p.4, Montgomery. Unpublished).

Because the Africans who invented the Medew Netcher language used pictures to express their language it illustrates, by their use of animate and inanimate objects that they saw all of reality as Divine.

For our purposes we have to broaden our understanding of Netcher, 𓊹. The standard translation of Netcher is God (p.576, Gardiner. 1994), and Gods for the plural form Netcheru, 𓊹𓊹𓊹, (p.59, Gardiner. 1994). The term God has become the standard way to translate Netcher because of the Christian, European cultural background of the early translators. This European God concept is an agreed upon translation of Netcher, 𓊹. However, that does not mean that the two concepts are equal. The concept of God is perhaps as close as the western mind can come to understanding the concept of Netcher, 𓊹, in one word.

The Netcher, 𓊹, and the Netcheru, 𓊹𓊹𓊹, can also be understood as principles. The Netcher, 'Wsir,' 𓊨, (Osiris), represents among others things, the concepts of resurrection and eternal life. For example: When 'Wsir' 𓊨, is referred to as the God of the Dead (p.562, Gardiner. 1994), an understanding of his functions is missed. 'Wsir' 𓊨, is the judge of the Dead who gives eternal life to the deceased. 'Wsir', 𓊨, also represent the cyclical, male regenerative aspect of nature and the spiritual continuity of personal consciousness after physical death. The Netcher and Netcheru operate as functional primary principals or archetypes powers of nature (p.548, Obenga. 2004).

The Netcheru, 𓊹𓊹𓊹, as concepts which express Divine Principles or archetypes destroys the ill-informed argument that Kemet was a polytheistic or monotheistic culture. (Why is the concept of a Monotheistic God considered advancement over the Polytheistic Gods concept? If one God is good, why is having more than one God, not more of that goodness, oh I forgot, some Gods are jealous!)

The study of the language of any culture turns into an attempt to understand how that culture thinks, and how they express those thoughts. The concepts expressed in the Mdw Ntr, 𓌃𓏛, Medew Netcher, (spelled with vowels) language illustrates an African culture whose ideas and thoughts were based on understanding the divine nature of reality and how to develop and bring out the divine nature of the individual.

Medew Nefer, 𓌃𓏺, Good Speech and, 𓐙, Maat

> We must stop misinterpreting words. We have misinterpreted words and have been the victim of the tyranny of words for all too long...We have fallen for the words, multi-cultural and multi-ethnic. The danger here is that the use of these terms gives the impression that some group created a high culture, and others fall in line behind them. It is the concept of the world waiting in darkness for Europe to bring the light, when the absolute truth is the contrary. Everywhere Europe went in this world, everywhere they invaded, they put out the light of the people's culture, and declared War on their way of life, their god, their language and their dress. *Dr. John H. Clarke*

Medew Netcher, 𓌃𓊹, (Divine Words) and Medew Nefer, 𓌃𓏺, (Good Speech, Good-words) are related concepts. In Kemet, all Principles (Netcheru) have relationships with other Principles. The stories of the Netcheru, 𓊹𓊹𓊹, demonstrate this point. The Netcheru, 𓊹𓊹𓊹, are represented as family members engaged in intense, intimate, volatile, peaceful and loving relationships to illustrate the interconnectivity and close relationship between the Principles, the Netcheru, 𓊹𓊹𓊹. Therefore we will have to examine other Principles of Kemet's culture to better understand the concept of Medew Nefer, 𓌃𓏺, Good Speech, from their perspective!

The concept of Medew Nefer, 𓌃𓏺, Good Speech, comes from a cultural worldview in which the goal was to nurture and develop the Divine, 𓊹, aspect of reality, humanity only being one aspect. This was accomplished by aligning the government and the individual's behavior to the concept of Maat (truth, righteousness, justice, fair and honest behavior). In the book, *Icons of Maat,* Egyptologist Theophile Obenga produces the following information, showing how the concept of Maat was interwoven throughout this ancient African society.

> Maat is concerned with all the spheres of reality. There are five realities:
> The divine or sacred world
>
> The Cosmos or the universe
>
> The state or the governance

> The society or the human community (humanity)
>
> The human being (family)
>
> Each of these realities has five dimensions of significance:
>
> Religious
>
> Cosmic
>
> Political
>
> Social
>
> Anthropological
>
> Thus, the five realities have together 125 dimensions of significance. This is Maat's number. It means that because of Maat, the sacred world must be balanced to itself, to the cosmos, to the state, to the society and to humans. The cosmos must be balanced to the divine world, to itself, to the state, to the society and to humans. The state must be balanced to the sacred, to the cosmos, to itself, and to humans. The humans must be balanced to the divine world, to the cosmos, to the state, to the society, and to themselves.(p.93-4, Obenga.1996)

The above quote by Dr. Obenga illustrates how all aspects of human activity were aligned with the concept of Maat. This Maatian way of life for the King and the individual enable them to reproduce the divine work of the Netcheru in the person and the society. The concept of Maat is a higher form of governance than democracy. It was the root concept of a society that existed longer than any other in known history.

Dr. Obenga goes on to show the importance of speech in incorporating such a lofty concept as Maat in the life of Kemetic society.

> In sum, Divine speech is the gift of the Creator to human beings. Kemetic tombs and iconographic panels explain that Amun gives All Life, Power and Health, Amun asserts, "I have given All Life, Power and Health like the Sun Forever." These are actions given meaning through speech, Human beings when acting as human beings relate through speech. Indeed, the Divine (i.e., gift) and the Good (i.e. Virtue) are linked through speech. One text asserts that "a man's mouth saves him" ("The Shipwrecked Sailor"). Other modes of relation such as beating or threatening or entic-

ing may achieve results but the truly human mode of behavior is commanded through speech. One is acting humanly only when one commands through speech, i.e., persuasion. Divine speech links humanity to divinity. Human beings learn and teach through Good Speech." (p.46, Obenga.2004)

This Maatian ordered Five realities (order being an attribute of Maat) indicates a precise ontological structural expression common to African culture. In Africa, the Sacred world is primary, first, and the foundation of the other four realties.

The above passage by Dr. Obenga also demonstrates that the people of Kemet understood the power of speech as rhetoric and as representative of one's character. It also states that being human means relating to other humans by speech. In Kemet and other parts of Africa, listening, discussion, debate and consensus are the humane way to solve deputes, not violence and the threat of it.

The concept of Medew Nefer, Good Speech, as conceptualized in this ancient society meant applying the principles of Maat to human speech. These Africans of the Hapy valley had an unimaginable amount of time to develop and perfect these cultural concepts. This is proven by the various Kings list carved and written on various temple walls and papyri that give statement to its long cultural history.

Djed Maat, 𓂋𓏤𓐍, Speaking Truth. Iri Maat, 𓁹𓐍, Doing Truth.
Medew Netcher, 𓏺𓊹, Good Speech.

> It becomes obvious that the people of the Hapi valley were not slaves to the King. The King's duty to do Maat was the same as the common person! The whole society was based on Divine concepts which demanded Good Speech and Good Behavior by all members. *A. Montgomery*

The concepts of Good Speech, Medew Nefer, 𓏺𓊹, Speaking Truth, Djed Maat 𓂋𓏤𓐍, Doing Truth, 'Iri' Maat, 𓁹𓐍, as practiced by the Africans of Kemet were developed as concepts one could use on a personal level to help the individual develop the divine aspects of their personality by aligning their behavior to Maat. Dr. Jacob Carruthers demonstrates how speech and behavior were based on each other.

> There is no alienation between speech and action. The definitive text on Maat, which Maulana Karenga entitled "Khun Anup" in the *Husia*, commands, "Speak Truth, Do Truth"; thus thinking and doing are inseparable. The relationship is symbolized through the divine concepts: *Sia, Hu* and *Heka*. Sia is the concept of exceptional intellectual clarity; Hu represents articulate command and Heka symbolizes extraordinary power. So indeed the mind thinks, the tongue orders and the body obeys-in that order. That is, when the minds sees with exceptional clarity, then the tongue speaks with authority and the limbs perform with extraordinary effectiveness and thus all good things come about; all great projects succeed. The command is obeyed when it is rightly conceived and articulately uttered because it is Truth (Maat)! (p.45, Carruthers. 1995)

In Kemet, it was not enough to just speak Truth, it was also necessary to do Truth or in their language, 'iri' Maat, 𓁹𓐍, Do Truth, and one way of doing truth was by demonstrating good behavior. Proper behavior was a primary focus of the Kemetic educational system. Good Speech without doing Maat (truth) did not exist in Kemet. Good speech must be followed by behavior based on doing right by being fair and respectful. This process served to developed individuals with discipline and self control.

The Creative Powers of Words

> Power is the ability to define reality and then have others respond to that definition as if it was their own. *Wade Nobles.*
>
> Words are one of the primary ways we (people) define reality to ourselves and each other. *A. Montgomery.*

The creation texts of Kemet are replete in detail with the use of speech as an aspect of creation. The following is Dr. Caruthers translations from the Shabaka Stone and the Coffin text of the Middle Kingdom. Dr. Carruthers analysis of these ancient African text are excellent, as he brings out the deep intellectual thought embedded within them.

For our purpose the beginning point is the epistemological statement in the text which encompasses the metaphysical theological basis as well. Let us first read the relevant part of the text from Breasted's transcript.

Sxm   ib   ns   m   awy

The power of the mind and tongue are in the limbs

mAA   irty   sDm   anxwy

The seeing of the eyes, the hearing of the ears, the

Ssnw   fnD   sar   snxr   ib ntf

Sniffing of the nose, are elevated to the mind, which

Dd   pr   arqty   nb

Causes every perception to come forth.

In ns wHm kAAt Hat(y) sw

Then the tongue repeats the thoughts of the mind; so

Ms nTrw nbw

all of the creative forces are born,

Itm pawt nTrw.f

Atum and his Primeval Powers.

These texts demonstrate that the people of Kemet had a precise understanding of the prime principles and causes of reality. The texts demonstrate that they understood how the senses forms an individual's perception. The text also demonstrates a realistic, practical view of reality, 'the limbs are the instruments for carrying out the desire and dictates of the mind.' These texts highlight the role of the mind and words in African metaphysical thought. Dr. Carruthers continues.

Sk xprn is mdw nTr nb m kaat hat(y)

All divine speech happened in the thoughts of the mind and the

wDwt ns...

commands of the tongue...

...mdt n

...The speech of the

kAAt ib prt m ns irrt

thinking mind comes forth from the tongue and makes

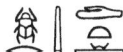

sm n xt nb

the specialization of everything...

mdw ntr nb

all speech is divine. (p. 42-3, Carruthers. 1999)

The Book of Maaa Kheru proclaims:

Xpr mdt

"when speech happened (came into beings)

nnk tm wnn wa kwi

the universe belong to me-I existed alone."

Ink Ra m haw.f tpw

I am Re in his first appearance,

wbn.f m axt

when he rises on the horizon

Ink ntr aA Xpr Ds.f

I am the Great God who happened himself

The same phenomenon is explained in the "Book of Knowing the Appearance of Re" Thusly:

Dd mdw nb r Dr Dd.f

Speech spoken: The Lord of the universe says;

Xpr.I   Xhr   Xprw

When I happen, happening itself happen

Hprw   kwi   m xprw   n   xpri

Thus I happen in the happening (advent) of the Happener

Xpr   m   sp tpy

Who happens on the First Occasion.

(Carruther's translation from Budge's text, 1969)

Summarizing the cosmic creation the Creator asserts:

After I happened

The happenings were abundant

Which came forth from my mouth.

...The role of creative speech is the emphasis of both texts.

(p. 47-9, Carruthers. 1999)

An understanding of the creative, transformative effect of words in relation to one's personality can be seen in western culture also. This same understanding is expressed in the concept of vocabulary building. Vocabulary or your personal lexicon of words used to conceptualize the world and express your thoughts, feelings and emotions.

Vocabulary building is encouraged in western culture to impress and influence others. Vocabulary use and word meanings are tested on western intelligence tests. The point being, that an internal base of the understanding, meaning and usages of different words has a positive influence on one's ability to understand and comprehend ideas. Vocabulary building, and more importantly reading, builds a personal internal base of words/concepts with which to draw upon to understand and interpret the world in which we interact. In other words, a strong vocabulary enhances the thinking process by broadening the conceptual base of one's internal dialogue.

Concepts which express the Divine nature of Words in Kemet.

MdwNtr; **Words are Divine**; they help to form and influence reality.

Mdw Nfr; **Good Speech**; practice Good Speech by learning the words of your elders and ancestors.

Djed Maat; **Speak Truth;** Try not to let words come form your mouth you have no intention of carrying out.

Iri Maat; **Do Truth.** Make your behavior match the truth of your words.

Shadi; means **Read and nourish.** Nourish the mind by reading books. Learn words/concepts which express African cultural concepts. These cultural concepts can be found in the life and works of African Nationalist scholars such as Edward W. Blyden, Henry H. Garnett, Hubert H. Harrison, France Fanon, Chiek A. Diop, Marimba Ani, Jacques Depelchin, Marcus M. Garvey Yoseff ben-Jochannan, Rkhty Amen-Jones, Francis Welsing and many others.

Hu; represents **articulate command.**

Sia; **Clear thinking,** the concept of exceptional intellectual clarity;

Clear thinking, is thinking based on the understanding of primary causes or principles and seeing how they operate in nature, and the ability to apply that understanding to life situations.

Heka; 𓉻𓂧𓁷 symbolizes **extraordinary power**. And in the words of Dr. Carruthers,... indeed the mind thinks, the tongue orders and the body obeys-in that order. That is, when the minds sees with exceptional clarity, then the tongue speaks with authority and the limbs perform with extraordinary effectiveness and thus all good things come about; all great projects succeed. The command is obeyed when it is rightly conceived and articulately uttered because it is Truth (Maat)! (p.45, Carruthers. 1995)

Conclusion

> Throw away the image of the god of the whites who has so often brought down our tears and listen to liberty which speaks in all our hearts. *Boukman Dutty*

Africans are correct to view words with such reverence. Based on the above information it becomes clear that the words we consume (put inside our selves) are just as important, if not more so, than the words we speak. After all, you can only repeat what you have taken in. This understanding highlights the need for African languages to become a larger component of the African centered school curriculum.

African languages must become a larger component as one of the tools used for personal, cultural and mental liberation. Languages are the product and conveyor of culture. Language represents a unique cultural way of conceptualizing and expressing reality. Language can be looked upon as the food of culture. To learn the language of a culture is to consume the ideas of that culture in their organic form.

To conceptualize words as nourishment means we must learn how to become as culturally critical of the **concepts** contained in the words we put into our minds as we do the food we put into our mouths. We are more conscious of the negative content of the food we eat than the **poisonous concepts** contained in the words we consume daily from the corporate owned mass media and institutionalized educational systems of European society.

The quote at the beginning of this section by Boukman Dutty, the obscure leader of the Haitian revolution, shows an awareness of the toxic content of western ideologies on Africans way back in 1791. This basic understanding and mistrust of Eurocentric beliefs has been educated out of most Africans. The result of consuming the ideas, concepts and beliefs fed to Black people by Eurocentric-Western educational institutions both secular and religious are illustrated by the ineffective, impotent nature of black social and political actions. Our present state of affairs is the logical, predictable outcome of years of toxic education.

The pernicious nature of this process is best documented in the book *"The Misedcuation of the Negro"* by Carter G. Woodson, published in 1933. This outstanding book also explains why the education we receive makes too many African-american educators recalcitrant to African cultural ideas.

To only consider food as the main component of health in connection to the body is based on outdated Newtonian "the universe as machine" physics. We must broaden our understanding of what we think being healthy is. The cultural nature of the ideas we consume must become a part of our understanding of health. We must consume more ideas and concepts of African culture to make them alive within us .

It is in African languages that we find words which contain cultural concepts of vital energy necessary for African intellectual sanity and physical wellbeing.

How would our health in bodies, mind and spirit respond if we consumed concepts contained in the words of MDW NTR or the words of the languages of the Bantu-Kongo, Zulu, Dogon or Yoruba and then used those concepts as the philosophical frameworks for the construction of our reality? What type of conceptual constructs could we bring into existence by using concepts found in African languages as ideological weapons against the inherited anti-African, non-nutritional value of concepts found in European thought and languages? This necessitates the need for the learning and use of African languages as vital food for African mental and cultural liberation. At the very least we must begin to consume and use philosophical concepts found in African culture to structure our lives upon.

Free Your Mind and Your Ass Will Follow,... George Clinton and the Funkadelics

Akinjide Bonotchi Montgomery
Of The Medew Netcher Study Group of Detroit.

Appendix
Medew Netcher: The use of Nature as Language

'sedgem'-Judge, Obey, Listen.

one of the most unique aspects of the Medew Netcher language (Ancient Egypt Hieroglyphics) is in its use of symbols of nature to express ideas. Along with expressing the phonetic value of a word the symbols also have a natural and cultural meaning. This use of objects enables them to layer a word with meaning by using the object itself to enforce the meaning. The objects themselves have an inherent meaning as objects of nature and a cultural meaning as manmade objects. The attributes of the animal and the use of the cultural object depicted were used to add meaning to words. The word 'sedgem' is the perfect example of this layered use. This word is translated as, to hear, obey, listen and judge. This word, 'sedgem' when written using the Mdw Ntr symbols consisted of two symbols, a cow's ear and an Owl. The phonetic value of these symbols are sdjm (with vowels, 'Sedgem')

The symbol of the Cow's ear being used for hearing is plain to see, but the owl allows for additional meaning to be uncovered by observing the actions of the Owl. The Owl is the perfect example of conserved energy, clammily and carefully analyzing by observing (looking and listening) to the environment. Waiting to unleash a silent, fast, precise and deadly amount of intensely focused energy. This understanding of the owl's attributes, 'presents this meaning for sedgem', to conserve energy, to focus, to analyze the environment by listening and observing in order to be more effective in future actions. Hence, the meaning of this word is enhanced by understanding the nature of the animals used to express the phonetic value of the word.

'sedgem' also implies that the people understood that to judge or to obey one must be a good listener.

This words and its use also denotes the educational, instructive nature of this African language. The language is constructed to reveal more about the words of the language, as the person learns more about the world around them.

Speech in man as creative power

Dr. H. E. Amadou Hampate Ba of Mali.

Maa Ngala, it is taught, deposited in Maa the three potentialities of ability, willing and knowing contained in the twenty components of which he was composed. But all the forces to which he is heir lie dumb within him. They are static, till speech comes and sets them into motion. Then, vivified by the divine Word, they begin to vibrate. At a first stage they become thoughts, at a second sound, and at a third word. Speech-spoken words- is therefore regarded as the materialization or externalization of the vibrations of forces.

Let me point out, though, that at this level the terms 'speaking' and 'listening' refer to realities far more vast than those we usually attribute to them. It is said: 'The speech of Maa Ngala is seen, is heard, is smelled, is tasted, is touched.' It is a total perception, a knowing in which the entire being is engaged.

In the same way, since speech is the externalization of the vibrations of forces, every manifestation of a force in any form whatever is to be regarded as its speech. That is why everything in the universe speaks: everything is speech that has taken on body and shape.

In Fulfulde, the word for 'speech' (haala) is derived from the verbal root hal, the idea of which is 'to give strength' and by extension 'to make material'. Fulani tradition teaches that Gueno, the Supreme Being, conferred strength on Kiikala, the first man, speaking to him. 'It was talking with God that made Kiikala strong', say the Silatiqui (the Fulani Master Initiates).

If speech is strength, that is because it creates a bond of coming-and-going (*yaawarta*, in Fulfulde) which generates movement and rhythm and therefore life and action. This movement to and fro is symbolized by the weaver's feet going up and down, as we shall see later in connection with the traditional crafts.(In fact the symbolism of the loom is entirely based in creative speech in action.)

In the image of Maaa Ngala's speech, of which it is an echo, human speech sets latent forces into motion. They are activated and aroused by speech-just as a man gets up, or turns, at the sound of his name.

Speech may create peace, as it may destroy it. It is like fire. One ill advised word may start a war just as one blazing twig may touch off a great conflagration. In

In Malian adage: 'What puts a thing into condition [that is, arranges it, disposes it favorably]? Speech. What damages a thing? Speech. What keeps a thing as it is? Speech. 'Tradition, then, confers on Kuma, the Word, not only creative power but a double function of saving and destroying. That is why speech, speech above all, is the great active agent of African magic. (p. 170-1, Ki-Zerbo, 1981).

Works cited

Ani, M. (1994). Yurugu; An African-centered Critique of European Cultural Thought and Behavior. Trenton, New Jersey.

Budge E.W. (1904). The Gods of the Egyptians: Studies in Egyptian Mythology. New York, United States of America. Dover Publications, Inc.

Clinton, G. (1970). Free Your Mind…And Your Ass Will Follow. Westbound records.

Carruthers, J. H. (1999). Intellectual Warfare: Chicago, IL. Third World Press.

Carruthers, J.H. (1995). Mdw Ntr Divine Speech: A Historiographical reflection of African Deep Thought from the Time of Pharaohs to the Present. London, UK. Karnak House.

Faulkner, R. A. (1988) A Concise Dictionary of Middle Egyptian. Oxford, England. Griffith Institute, Ashmolean Museum.

FU-Kiau, K. K. B. (2000) Tying The Spiritual Knot-African Cosmology of the Bantu-Kongo– Principles of Life & Living.

Gardiner, A. (1994). Egyptian Grammar: Being an introduction to the study of hieroglyphs. Oxford, England. Griffith Institute, Ashmolean Museum.

Ki-Zerbo, J. (1981) General History of Africa I: Methodology and African Prehistory. California, Untied States of America. University of California Press.

Lee,I. (2006). Brain Education for Enhanced Learning: Teacher Manual. BR Consulting, Inc. Sedona. AZ.

Montgomery, A. B (2008) Kheper the Process of Coming into Existence! . Lulu.com

Montgomery, A.B. (2005) Reswet (South) is Up or Why Africans live in a World Turned Upside Down. Lulu.com.

Obenga, T. (2004). African Philosophy The Pharaonic Period: 2780-330 BC. Per Ankh

Obenga, T. (1996). Icons of Maat. Philadelphia, Penn. The Source Editions.

Obenga, T. (2002) KMT Language Through Primary Texts: Original Data – Precise Examination – Comments. San Francisco, United States of America. Pillar Edition.

www.ingramcontent.com/pod-product-compliance
Lightning Source LLC
Chambersburg PA
CBHW041520220426
43667CB00002B/45